746.43
Ru   Rubenstone, Jessie
     Crochet for beginners. Photographs by
Edward Stevenson.   Philadelphia, Lippincott,
[1974]
     64p.   illus.

     1.Crocheting.   I.Stevenson, Edward, illus.
II.Title.

CROCHET FOR BEGINNERS

by Jessie Rubenstone

Photographs by Edward Stevenson

J. B. Lippincott Company / Philadelphia and New York

For Joan — my dear one

The author gratefully acknowledges the assistance of Mrs. Mary Merva of Hawk Run, Pennsylvania, who shared her discoveries about crocheting with plastic.

U.S. Library of Congress Cataloging in Publication Data

Rubenstone, Jessie.
  Crochet for beginners.

  SUMMARY: Describes the materials and basic stitches for the beginning crocheter and gives directions for making such crocheted items as a head-band, belt, pot holder, rug, poncho, and others.
    1. Crocheting — Juvenile literature. [1. Crocheting] I. Stevenson, Edward, illus. II. Title.
TT820.R778   746.4'3   74-4462
ISBN-0-397-31547-3   ISBN-0-397-31548-1 (pbk.)

Contents

So You Want to Crochet

Crochet (pronounced crow-SHAY) is a kind of needlework in which a hook called a *crochet hook* is used to catch the yarn and pull it through a loop. The crochet fabric is made by pulling one loop through another loop. This fabric stretches. It also unravels easily because the whole thing is one continuous thread.

Hand-crocheted articles are different from those that are made by machine and cost more when bought in a store. Hand-crocheted articles wear better, wash better, and last longer. It is easier to get just what you want when you crochet it yourself, because you can pick the color and style. The cost is much lower, too. The yarn used in hand-crocheted articles can be unraveled, washed, and used again (recycled).

In this book you will find directions for the basic crochet stitches and for some easy things to make. You may want to ask someone who knows how to crochet to help you follow these directions. With the skill you will develop, you will be able to make the more advanced projects you will find in other books.

Crochet gives you a chance to be creative. You have a wide choice of materials, colors, combinations of colors, and sizes. The directions for the articles pictured in this book will give you the finished size, but you can make most of them larger or smaller by changing the size of the crochet hook or the number of stitches. You can use up odds and ends of yarn to make beautiful crocheted articles that use small amounts. The colorful "granny squares" used in several projects in this book were made from many small pieces of yarn.

At first crochet may seem hard to do, but as you practice it will get much easier, and then you will really enjoy it. You will find that you can crochet while talking with friends or listening to the radio or watching television.

What You Will Need

You will need two things in order to crochet: a crochet hook and some yarn, string, or other crochet material.

CROCHET HOOKS

Crochet hooks are made of plastic, metal, wood, or bone. They come in different sizes (thicknesses), named by letters or numbers. We used a plastic crochet hook, size H, to make most of the articles in this book, but it is not necessary to use this size. You can get a good result with any size hook. Just be sure to use a hook that is not too thick or thin for your yarn. A smaller size (thinner) hook makes smaller stitches, so the finished article will be smaller. The thicker the hook, the larger the finished article.

CROCHET MATERIALS

YARN: Many kinds of yarn can be used for crochet. Yarn made from wool has always been popular. Wool yarn may be thick or thin, depending on the number of threads or *ply* that are twisted together to form the yarn. Three-ply yarn has three threads and four-ply yarn has four; four-ply yarn is thicker than three-ply.

Another popular yarn that is used today is made from synthetic (man-made) fibers like Acrilan, Orlon, or nylon. These yarns look like wool and may be used the same way. Rug yarn is heavy yarn usually made of a mixture of cotton and rayon. It is recommended for several projects in this book.

7

Yarn is sold in balls or skeins. Yarn in a *pull skein* can be pulled out without tangling and is easy to use. If the skein is not a pull skein, the yarn must be made into a ball to keep it from getting tangled as you use it.

It is important to read the label when buying yarn. Some or all of the following information is on the label:

Fiber or fibers used (cotton, nylon, Orlon, wool, etc.)

Weight—given in ounces

Length—given in feet or yards

Ply (number of threads plied together)

Color—number of color and number of dye lot. A *dye lot* is a batch of yarn that is dyed at the same time. Buy all of the yarn needed for an article at one time. Be sure the dye lot number is the same. Yarn from different dye lots will not match exactly even if the color may look the same. If you have a whole skein left over, it may be returned to the store.

STRING: String is usually made of cotton fibers. Other names for string are *twine* and *cord.* It is sold in balls.

PLASTIC: Don't throw away those plastic bags! You can crochet with plastic if you cut it into strips. This material does not cost anything. We also help protect the environment if we recycle plastic instead of adding to the pollution problem.

Plastic has many good qualities for use in the house. A rug made of plastic will not slip on the floor. Plastic does not absorb dirt and does not have to be washed very often. It is easy to clean; just wipe plastic articles with a damp cloth or swish in warm water with a little detergent. Plastic is strong and will last a long time.

All kinds of plastic bags may be used, but they have different qualities. Some are heavier than others. Some will be easy to work with and some may stick to the crochet hook. Experiment to find the kind you like. Bread bags and trash bags are easy to crochet with.

Plastic for crocheting must be cut into one long strip. You can do this by cutting around and around a plastic bag. Starting at one end, take scissors and cut into the bag on a slant until the strip is the right width. Then, using a small ruler or a piece of cardboard as a measure to check the width occasionally, continue cutting until you get to the other end of the bag. The strips do not have to be perfectly even.

Crochet plastic as you would crochet yarn or string. If it sticks to the crochet hook, put a little Vaseline (or any kind of oil or grease) on the hook, and the plastic will work smoothly without sticking. Never use heat on plastic; heat will melt it. NEVER IRON PLASTIC.

OTHER MATERIALS: Many other materials may be used for crochet. You can crochet with ribbon or straw fibers. Nylon stockings can be cut into one-inch strips and made into beautiful rugs. Follow the directions for the plastic rug. One-inch strips of cloth may be used the same way. Join the nylon or cloth strips together by sewing. Wind this "yarn" into a ball before starting to crochet.

In addition to a crochet hook and yarn, you will find the following things useful:

A *tapestry needle,* a thick sewing needle with a large eye and a rounded point. It is used to sew crochet together. You can also use it to hide ends of yarn by weaving them in and out of nearby stitches. A darning needle may also be used for this.

A *ruler* or tape measure.

Scissors for cutting yarn.

WHERE TO BUY SUPPLIES

Crochet hooks may be bought in five-and-ten-cent stores, yarn shops, or the "Art Needlework" department of department stores. A size H plastic crochet hook costs about thirty cents.

Yarn and string may be bought in the same places. Another good place to buy string is a hardware store. Large food markets also sell yarn and string. Shop around when you buy these things. Sometimes stores have sales or special values. Check the labels carefully for information.

Making the Sample

Before you start to crochet any of the things in this book, be sure you can make a good sample. Even if you can crochet, you should follow the directions and make the sample. You may use any kind of yarn or string and any size crochet hook. The sample includes all the stitches you will need for making the articles in this book.

Practice is important in learning any new skill. Practice making the sample until it is right. Do not expect your crochet to look perfect. Only work that is done by machine looks perfect. Practice each step until you feel comfortable.

Hold the yarn in your left hand as shown in the picture. Holding the yarn over the first finger (forefinger) and between the last two fingers helps you to control

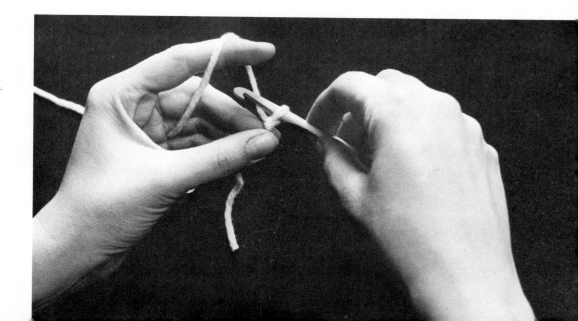

the tension (tightness) of the yarn. You will also hold onto your work near the crochet hook with the thumb and middle finger of the left hand, as shown.

There are several ways to hold the crochet hook. The picture shows the easiest way. Practice holding it this way until it feels comfortable in your right hand. Note that the hook faces down, though you will turn it slightly to catch the yarn.

Left-handed persons should follow these same directions. If you are left-handed, you may find this hard at first. However, you probably hold a spoon or a knife in your right hand when eating, and the crochet hook is held very much the same way. Both hands are used to crochet. Left-handed persons will find that they move the left hand more, and right-handed persons will find that they do more of the work with the right hand.

CHAIN STITCH

The basic stitch in crochet is called the *chain stitch.* A row of these stitches is called a *chain*, which is what it looks like. Making a chain is the first step in every crochet project. Starting on p. 14, follow the directions under each picture and do one step at a time.

The yarn must be loose when the hook pulls it through the loop. If you pull it tight, the loop will be too small for the hook to go through. After the yarn is pulled through the loop, tighten the loop a *little* by lifting your forefinger. Do not pull the loop tight, as the crochet hook must be able to slide through easily. It is a good idea to keep your chain very loose when you begin to crochet. When you get the feel of it, it will be easy to make the stitches tighter.

As you push the crochet hook through the loop to catch the yarn, be sure the thickest part of the crochet hook goes through the loop. This will help make your work even.

Always hold the chain with the thumb and middle finger of the left hand. Hold your work close to the crochet hook. As you crochet, you must keep moving these fingers along so that they are always holding the work close to the crochet hook.

Count the stitches as you make them. When you finish the chain, go back and count them again to make sure you have the right number. Do not count the slip knot or the loop on the hook.

After you have made a chain, remove the crochet hook and pull both ends of the yarn. You will find that you have ripped out the whole chain. Make another one. Continue to practice making chains until your work is even. Stitches should be the same size. When you can make a good chain, you will be able to learn the other stitches easily.

For the sample, make a chain of 16 stitches. Another way to say this is "chain 16."

1. Before you start making your chain, you need a loop on your crochet hook. This first loop is called a slip knot. To make it, form a loop by crossing the yarn. Note that the short end is on the bottom. Put the crochet hook into the loop.

2. Catch the long end of the yarn with the crochet hook and pull it up through the loop.

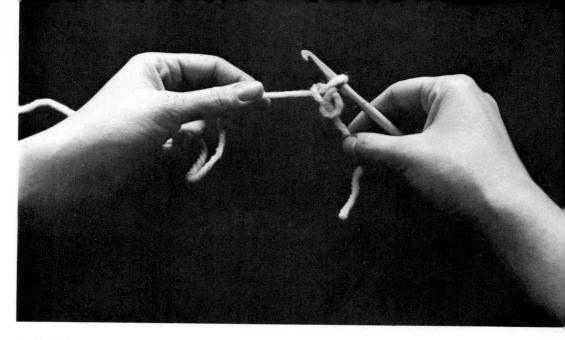

3. Pull both ends of the yarn to make the loop smaller. It should be loose enough to slide easily along the crochet hook. You have completed your slip knot.

4. For chain stitch, hold the crochet hook in front of the yarn.

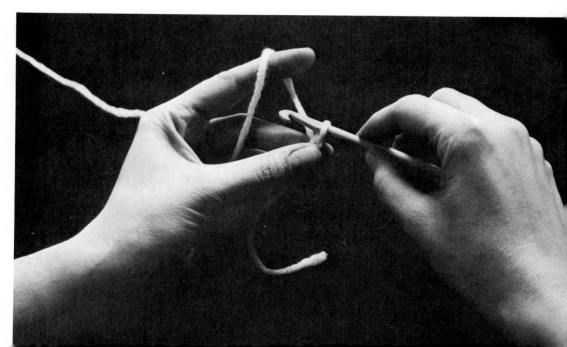

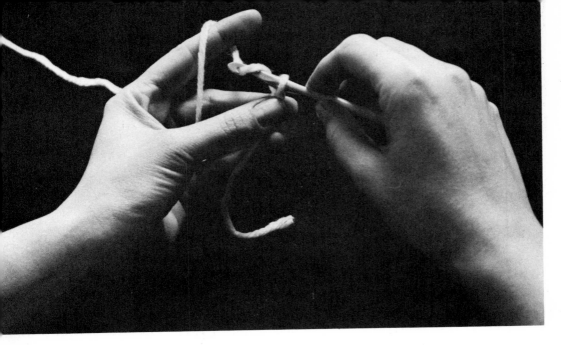

5. Wrap the yarn over the hook.

6. Catch the yarn with the hook...

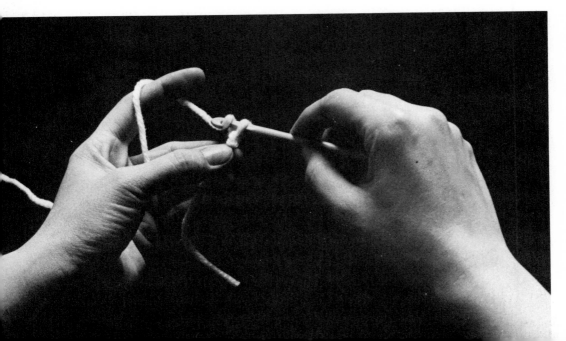

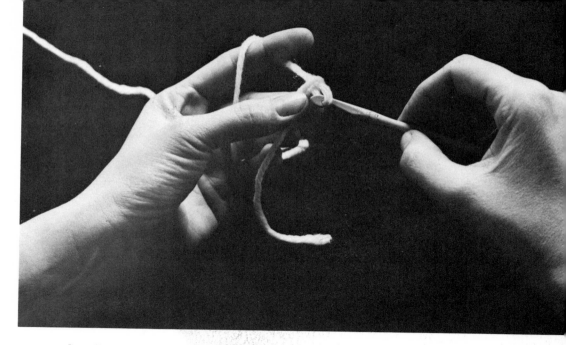

. . . and pull it through the loop. The new loop should slide easily along the thickest part of the crochet hook. Return hook to starting position.

You have made your first chain stitch.

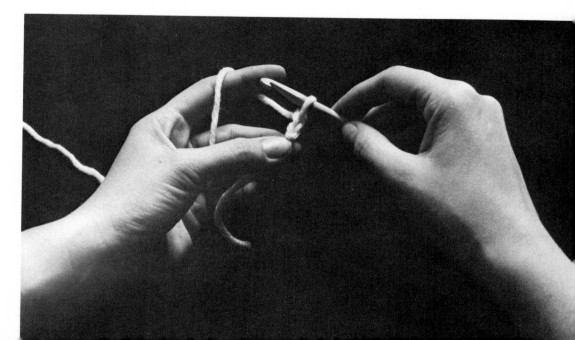

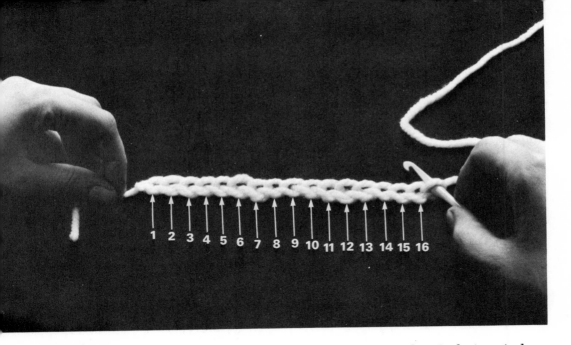

Repeat steps 4, 5, and 6 until you have made 16 chain stitches. Keep the chain flat as you work. Do not twist it.

COUNT THE STITCHES. Do not count the slip knot. Do not count the loop on the crochet hook.

SINGLE CROCHET

You have made the basic chain of 16 stitches. For single crochet, follow the pictures and directions and do one step at a time. Keep the chain flat. Do not twist it.

You are going to crochet back and forth in rows, turning your work at the end of each row to work back the other way. At the end of the first row of single crochet, stop and count the stitches. If you do not have 16 stitches, you have made a mistake. Rip it out and do it again.

For the sample, work 4 rows of single crochet.

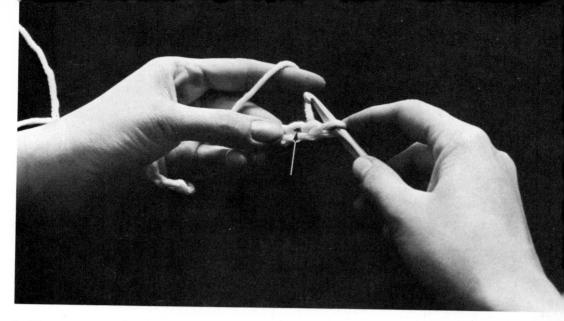

1. To start a row of single crochet, work 1 chain stitch. (You now have 17 chain stitches.) You must work 1 chain stitch before beginning every row of single crochet. For the first stitch, you will skip one chain stitch and put the crochet hook into the second chain stitch from the hook. In a single crochet row worked on a chain, the first stitch is always made in the second chain stitch from the hook.

2. Put the crochet hook into the chain stitch from the front and under *one* top thread.

3. Wrap the yarn over the hook. Catch the yarn and pull it through the chain stitch. You now have two loops on the hook.

4. Wrap the yarn over the hook again. Catch the yarn and pull it through both the loops on the crochet hook.

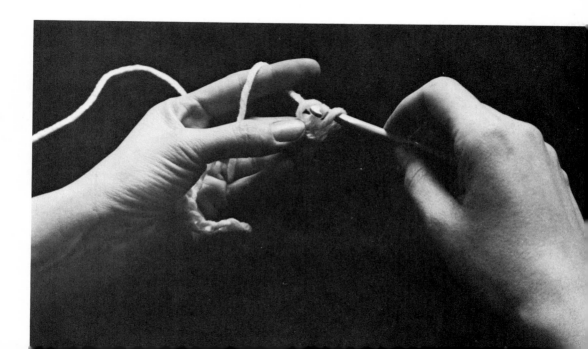

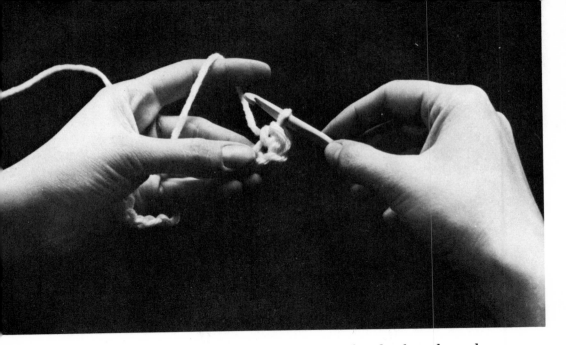

You now have one loop on the crochet hook and you have completed one single crochet stitch.

Repeat steps 2, 3, and 4 to make a single crochet stitch in each chain stitch until you reach the end of the chain. You have finished 1 row of single crochet. Stop and count your stitches. You should have 16.

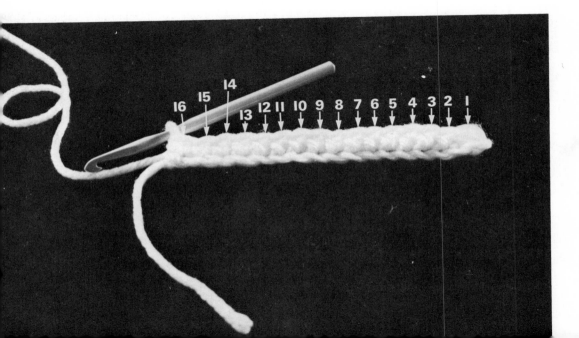

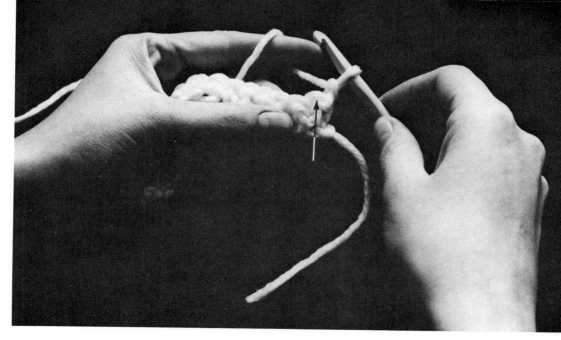

5. Make 1 chain stitch (as you did in step 1) and turn your work so the crochet hook is on the right.

6. Put the crochet hook into the first stitch (which is the last stitch of the row before). For each single crochet stitch in this row and in all rows after the first, put the crochet hook under the top *two* threads of the stitch, then do steps 3 and 4.

Be sure to chain 1 before turning your work to begin a row of single crochet.

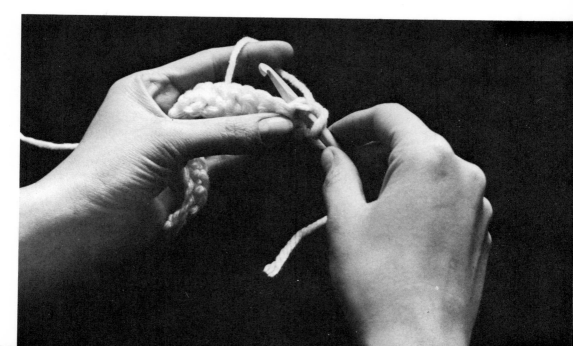

DOUBLE CROCHET

Double crochet is done much like single crochet, but it makes a higher stitch because you pull the yarn through more loops. Follow the pictures and directions and do one step at a time.

When you reach the end of a row, count the stitches. Double crochet stitches are easy to count because they are so high.

For the sample, work 4 rows of double crochet.

1. To start a row of double crochet, *work 3 chain stitches*. This chain is the first stitch of the double crochet row. Turn your work so the crochet hook is on the right.

In double crochet you skip the first stitch of the row. You will put the crochet hook into the second stitch from the hook.

2. Wrap the yarn over the hook.

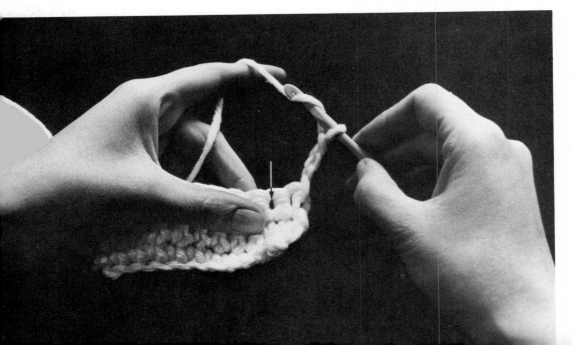

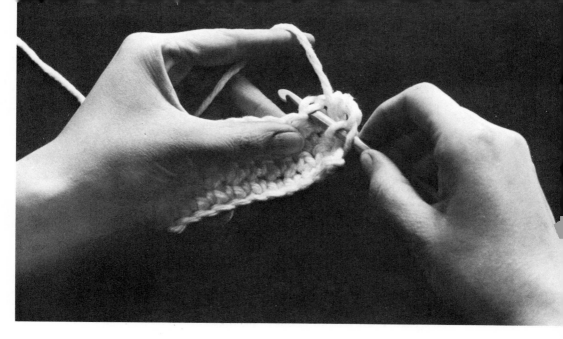

3. Put the crochet hook under the top *two* threads of the stitch.

4. Wrap the yarn over the hook again. Catch the yarn with the crochet hook . . .

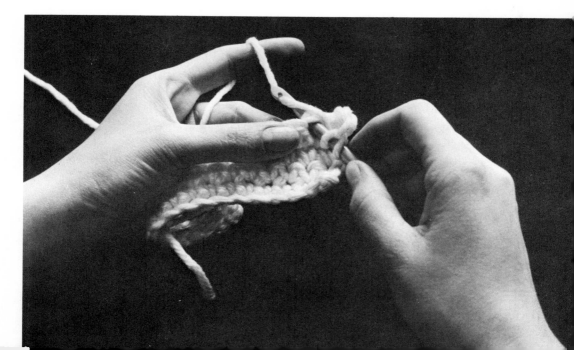

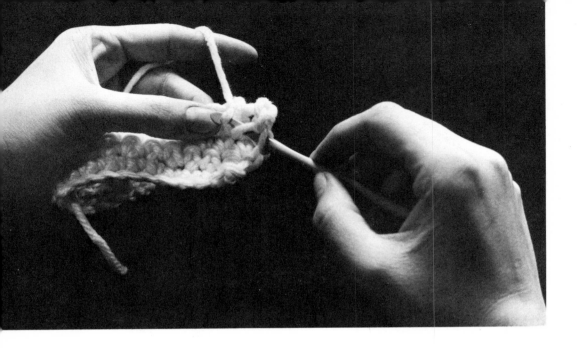

. . . and pull it through the stitch. You now have three loops on the crochet hook.

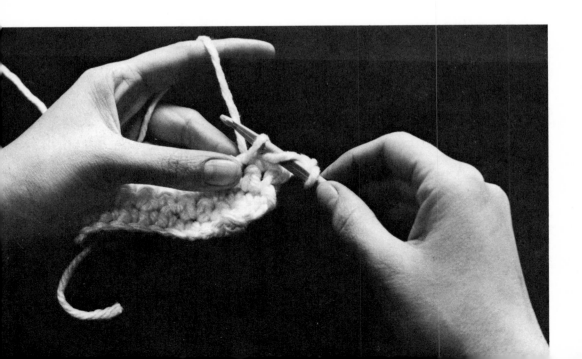

5. Wrap the yarn over the hook again. Catch the yarn and pull it through the first two loops only.

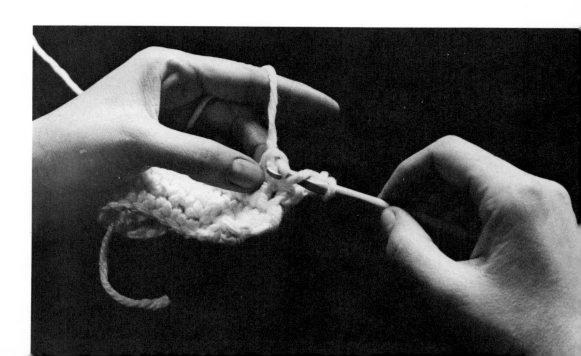

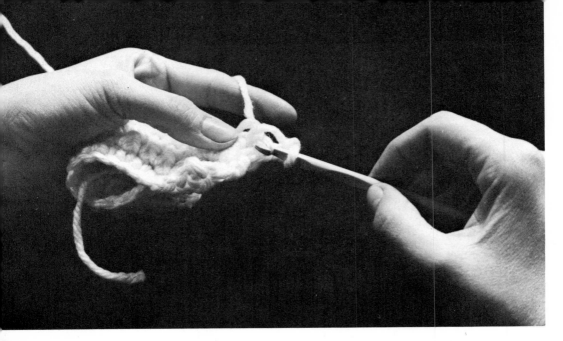

You now have two loops on the crochet hook.

6. Wrap the yarn over the hook again and pull it through the remaining two loops on the hook.

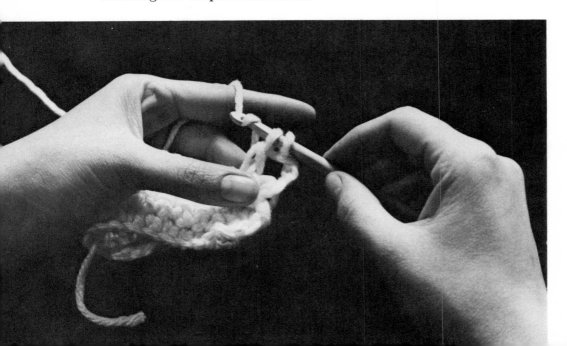

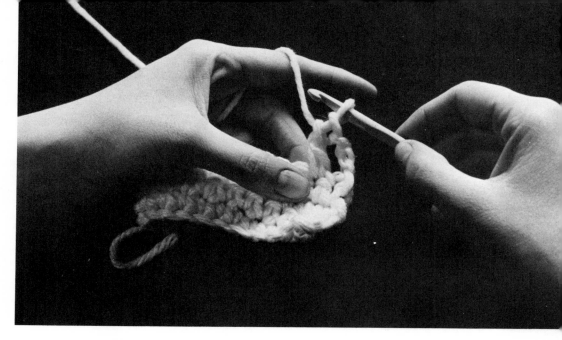

You now have one loop on the crochet hook. You have completed one double crochet stitch, the second stitch of the row.

Repeat steps 2, 3, 4, 5, and 6 to make a double crochet stitch in each stitch until you reach the end of the row. If the row before was a double crochet row, the last stitch is made by putting the hook into the top of the chain 3 that was the first stitch of that row. Count your stitches.

Be sure to chain 3 before turning your work to begin a row of double crochet, and be sure to skip the first stitch.

ENDING OFF

At the end of the work, cut the yarn, leaving an end a few inches long. If the piece is to be joined to another piece, leave a long enough end to join it with. Use the crochet hook to pull this end through the last stitch. Pull tight to fasten.

You have completed the sample. There should be 16 stitches in every row. You should be in the habit of counting them as you work.

Now that you can crochet, you can make all the things in this book.

ABBREVIATIONS

An abbreviation is a short form of a word. Abbreviations are used in directions for crochet. In this book, the following abbreviations are used:

ch	chain or chain stitch	oz	ounce or ounces
dc	double crochet	sc	single crochet
in	inch or inches	st	stitch

*   This mark is called an *asterisk*. Instructions between two asterisks are to be repeated a certain number of times. For example,

3 dc in next st, ch 1 four times

means: "Work 3 double crochet stitches in the next stitch and then work 1 chain stitch, then do both of these things three more times."

The directions for making the sample you have just completed would look like this:

SAMPLE

Crochet hook   Any size
Yarn   Any kind

Ch 16.
Sc for 4 rows.
Dc for 4 rows. End off.

The directions will *not* remind you to make 1 chain stitch before each row of single crochet or to make 3 chain stitches as the first stitch in each row of double crochet. Be sure you chain 1 before turning your work to do a row of single crochet and chain 3 before turning your work to do a row of double crochet.

SIZES AND MEASURING

In the directions that follow, the size of the crochet hook and the kind of yarn are given. The finished size is based on this size hook and yarn. Feel free to experiment by changing these. Use your own ideas. If you make a mistake, it is easy to rip crochet and to pick up the loop again.

When you measure your work, lay it on a flat surface like a table or the floor. Do not stretch the crochet when measuring unless the directions tell you to.

Articles to Crochet

HEADBAND

Crochet hook   Size H
Yarn   ½ oz, 4-ply wool
Size   1 in x 16 in (or size that fits your head)

Ch 4.

Work back and forth in sc. Each row should have 4 stitches.

Continue to work until it is the size you want. Measure it on your head as you work. It should be a little smaller than your head size, as it will stretch.

When it is long enough, end off, leaving a long end of yarn to join it together. Join the short ends together following directions below.

TO SEW TWO CROCHETED PIECES TOGETHER: Pin the two edges together evenly. Thread a tapestry needle with the same yarn that was used in making the article. If yarn is not attached to the work, fasten it well at the beginning of the seam by taking two or three stitches in the same place.

Work from side to side, taking small stitches in the edges, as shown. Try to keep the seam flat.

Fasten the yarn at the end of the seam by taking two or three stitches in the same place so that it does not show.

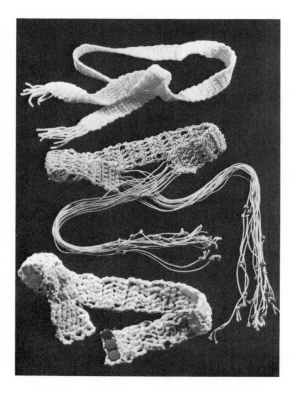

Yarn belt

String belt

Plastic belt

YARN BELT

Crochet hook	Size H
Yarn	1 oz, 4-ply wool
Size (including fringe)	1¼ in x 50 in
Fringe	10 pieces of yarn, 6 inches long

Cut the yarn for the fringe before starting to crochet the belt. Set it aside until the belt is finished.

Ch 5.

Work back and forth in sc. Every row should have 5 stitches. Continue to work until it is the length you want. The belt in the picture measured 46 inches before the fringe was added. End off.

Add fringe, following directions below.

FRINGE: The fringe is pulled through the stitches at the short ends of the belt.

Put the crochet hook through the first stitch and catch the center of the piece of yarn. Pull it halfway through. This will form a loop (*a*). Put the crochet hook through this loop, catch the two ends of yarn (*b*), and pull

(*a*)

(*b*)

through the loop. Pull tight (c). Repeat this for each stitch along both ends.

(c)

If you need only a few pieces of fringe, it is easy to measure and cut them the same length. To cut many pieces, wind yarn around pieces of cardboard as in making a tassel (p. 50). Remember that the finished fringe will be a little less than half as long as the pieces of yarn you cut.

You may use one or more pieces of fringe in each stitch, or use two or three pieces of yarn in every other stitch. Beads may be put on the fringe; knot the yarn to hold the beads in place. Or the articles may be made without fringe.

STRING BELT

Crochet hook	Size H
Yarn	String of any kind. The belt in the picture was made from a 35-cent ball
Size (including fringe)	1½ in x 65 in

Ch 6.

Sc for 3 rows. You should have 6 stitches.

Dc next row and continue to work in dc until belt measures about 4 inches less than your waist. This belt will stretch; when you are measuring it, stretch it. When the belt is the size you want, sc for 3 rows. End off.

Divide the remaining string into 12 pieces of equal length. Use these pieces for the fringe, following directions on p. 35. The fringe on this belt is long enough to tie the belt together. Beads may be added.

PLASTIC BELT

Crochet hook	Size H
Yarn	½-inch strips of plastic
Size	2 in x 25 in (or size that fits your waist)

Follow instructions for string belt, making belt fit your waist measurement.

After the last row of sc, chain 5, skip 2 stitches, and join to next stitch with a slip stitch (see below). This forms a buttonhole. Make two more buttonholes the same way. End off. Sew three buttons to the other end of the belt.

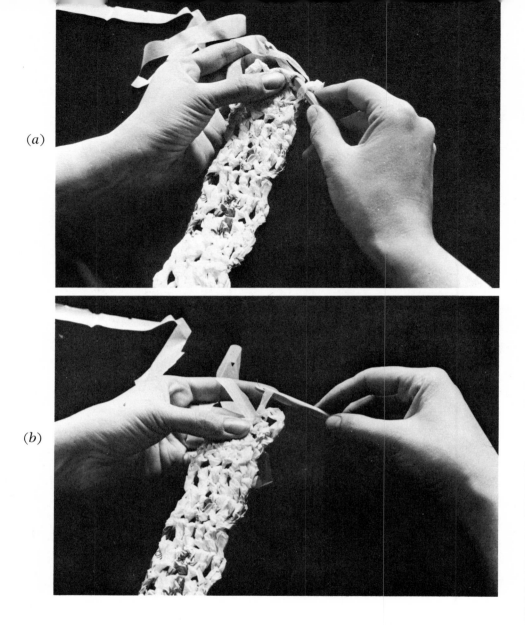

(a)

(b)

TO JOIN WITH SLIP STITCH: With one loop on the hook, put the hook into the stitch you wish to join to (a). Catch the yarn and pull it through both loops on the hook, leaving one loop on the hook (b).

Small scarf (left),
large scarf (right)

SMALL SCARF

Crochet hook	Size H
Yarn	4 oz, 4-ply wool
Size (including fringe)	5 in x 64 in
Fringe	20 pieces of yarn, 12 inches long

This scarf can be made from one 4-oz skein of yarn. Cut the fringe first and set it aside. Use the rest of the yarn to crochet the scarf.

Ch 16.

Sc for 1 row.

Dc every row until most of the yarn is used. Every row should have 16 stitches.

Sc for 1 row. End off.

Add fringe, following directions on p. 35. The sample has two pieces of fringe in five places spaced evenly along each end.

LARGE SCARF

Crochet hook	Size H
Yarn	9 oz, 4-ply wool
Size (including fringe)	10 in x 84 in
Fringe	136 pieces of yarn, 20 inches long

Ch 33.

Sc for 1 row.

Dc every row until the scarf is as long as you want. Every row should have 33 stitches.

Sc for 1 row. End off.

Add fringe, following directions on p. 35. The scarf in the picture has four pieces of fringe in every other stitch.

This scarf was made with three colors of yarn. You will have to join a new piece of yarn when you change colors or when you use up a ball of yarn.

TO JOIN A NEW PIECE OF YARN: Lay end of new yarn over end of old yarn and crochet the next stitch with both pieces. Then use only the new yarn. Hide the cut ends of yarn by working the next stitches over them, or wait until you have finished the article and hide the ends by pulling them through nearby stitches with a crochet hook. When changing to a different color, it is a good idea to add the new yarn at the end of a row to make an even stripe.

POT HOLDERS

Crochet hook	Size H
Yarn	1/3 oz, rug yarn
Size: plain	5½ inches square
with border	6 inches square

Ch 16.

Work in sc until piece is square (as long as it is wide).

For plain pot holder, do not end off. Ch 10 for loop and join to same corner with slip stitch (p. 38). End off.

For pot holder with border, end off at end of square. Finish edge with sc following directions below. A different color will look nice. After working sc all the way around, ch 10 for loop and join to same corner with slip stitch. End off.

TO FINISH EDGE WITH SINGLE CROCHET: Put the crochet hook through the first stitch after the corner. Catch the new yarn and pull it through to form a loop (*a*). Then catch the two ends in back and pull them through the loop (*b*). Using only the long piece of yarn, ch 1 and work sc along the edge. Hold the short end along the edge and crochet over it to hide it (*c*).

(*a*)

(*b*)

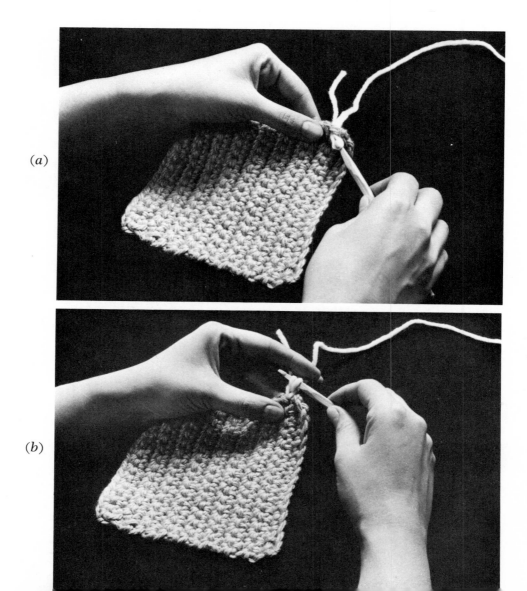

(c)

To turn corner, work 3 sc in the corner stitch.

When you have worked all the way around, join to the first stitch of the border with slip stitch (p. 38). End off. For a wider border, do not end off after making the slip stitch. Ch 1 and work another row of sc all the way around. Repeat until border is the width you want. Remember to make 3 stitches in each corner stitch.

PLASTIC PLACE MAT

Crochet hook   Size H
Yarn   1-inch strips of plastic
Size   11 in x 17 in

Any kind of plastic may be used. The mat in the picture was made from plastic bread wrappers.

Ch 25.

Sc until piece measures 15 inches. End off.

Work 2 rows of sc around mat, following directions on p. 42.

YARN RUG

Crochet hook	Size J
Yarn	4 skeins (single) or 8 skeins (double), rug yarn
Size	18 in x 27 in

This rug may be made with the yarn single or double. Double yarn makes a heavier rug. To use the yarn double, roll it into balls and work with two balls at the same time. Both may be the same color, or you can get a pretty tweed by mixing two colors or two shades of the same color.

Yarn rug (left),
plastic rug (right)

Ch 38.

Sc until piece measures 26 inches. End off.

Work sc around edge, using the same color or a contrasting color, following directions on p. 42. End off.

PLASTIC RUG

Follow directions for yarn rug, using 2-inch strips of plastic. For a tweed effect, use two 1-inch strips of different colors.

BEAN BAG AND PINCUSHION

Crochet hook	Size H
Yarn	1 oz, rug yarn
Size	5 inches square

Ch 16.

Work in sc until piece is square. End off.

Make another square following these same directions. It can be a different color.

Crochet the squares together following the directions below. Stop crocheting about halfway along the last side, leaving crochet hook in work. For bean bag, fill the

opening with dried beans of any kind. For pincushion, stuff firmly with foam rubber, old nylon stockings, or rags. Continue to work sc to the end of the opening. End off.

To add fringe to the pincushion, cut 16 pieces of yarn 6 inches long. If you have used two colors, use some of each color. Put 4 pieces in each corner following directions for fringe on p. 35.

TO CROCHET TWO PIECES TOGETHER: Pin the edges together evenly. Work sc along the edges to be joined, as if you were finishing the edge with sc (p. 42), but make sure the crochet hook goes through a stitch of both pieces to start every stitch. If the seam goes around a corner, work 3 sc in the corner stitch.

BABY BLOCKS

Crochet hook   Size H
Yarn   4-ply wool (small amounts depending on size of blocks)
Size   3 inches, 3½ inches, and 4 inches square

These blocks may be made any size. The blocks in the picture were made from squares with 10, 12, and 14 stitches.

Using sc, make 6 squares of the same size for each block. Use different colors of yarn.

To put blocks together, start by pinning two squares together along one edge. Join them following directions on p. 46. Use a contrasting color of yarn for joining the squares. Do not end off after joining one seam, but let the crochet hook remain in place while you pin on another square. You will be able to join several squares with one continuous piece of yarn, but you will have to end off and start again to be able to join all the squares together. Leave one side of the block open so that the stuffing may be put inside.

Stuff block firmly with rags or nylon stockings. Join the last two edges together.

HAT

Crochet hook	Size H
Yarn	2 oz, 4-ply wool
Size	Fits most sizes

Ch 14.

Sc for 1 row.

Dc for 7 rows.

Sc for 1 row. End off.

The finished piece should be a square, measuring about 4½ inches on each side. Make four more of these. Four squares are used to go around the head and the fifth is on top. Crochet the squares together, following directions on p. 46. Use a contrasting color of yarn.

The hat in the picture has two rows of sc around the bottom. Try the hat on before you start to make this

48

border. If you would like it tighter, skip a stitch a few times as you work around the row, or use a smaller size crochet hook. Try it on as you go along. You may have to rip this edge and do it again to get the size that you want.

With contrasting color, work 2 rows of sc (or more if you wish). Join to first stitch of last row with a slip stitch (p. 38). End off.

DRAWSTRING BAG

Crochet hook	Size H
Yarn	3 oz, 4-ply wool
Size (including fringe)	8 in x 12 in
Fringe	30 pieces of yarn, 6 inches long

Ch 30.
Sc for 8 inches.

Dc for 1 row.

Sc for 4 rows. End off.

This piece will measure 8 inches wide by 9 inches long. Make another piece following the same directions. Put the two pieces together, making sure the dc rows match. This end will be the top of the bag. Pin the other three sides together, leaving the top open. Crochet the pieces together, following directions on p. 46.

Attach fringe to the bottom of the bag, following the directions for fringe on p. 35.

For drawstrings, make 2 chains, each 30 inches long. Leave enough yarn at both ends of each chain to attach to a tassel. Pull the chains through the double crochet row, going under 2 stitches and over 2 stitches as shown. Note that both chains go through the same spaces but the ends come out on opposite sides.

Make 2 tassels following directions below. Tie both ends of each chain to a tassel. Hide the ends of yarn by pulling them through the tassel.

TASSEL: Take 2 strips of cardboard about 3 inches wide. Wind yarn around them 16 times. Pull an 8-inch piece of yarn between the pieces of cardboard (*a*) with a crochet hook and tie it securely at the top. Slide one blade of a scissors between the pieces of cardboard and cut through the strands at the bottom (*b*). Wind another 8-inch piece of yarn tightly around the tassel about ¾ inch from the top and knot it tightly (*c*). Hide the ends by pulling them inside the tassel with the crochet hook.

Tassels may be made in different sizes. The size depends on the width of the cardboard and the number of times the yarn is wound around it. Do not make a tassel too thick, as it will be hard to wind the yarn around the top.

PONCHO

Crochet hook	Size H
Yarn	16 oz, 4-ply wool
Size	Fits most sizes

Ch 60.

Sc for 1 row.

Dc until piece measures 32 inches.

Sc for 1 row. End off.

Finished piece should measure about 20 inches by 32 inches. Make another piece following the same directions.

Pin the two pieces together as shown and sew, following directions on p. 33.

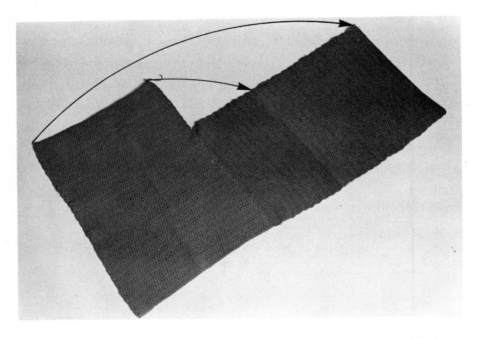

For drawstring, make a chain 60 inches long. Weave this in and out of the stitches around the neck as shown. Make 2 pompons following directions below. Tie them to the ends of the drawstring.

POMPON: Take 2 strips of cardboard 1 inch wide. Wind yarn around them 100 times. Pull an 8-inch piece of yarn between the pieces of cardboard and tie it securely at the top. Cut through the strands at the bottom. Pompons can be made in any size, depending on the width of the cardboard and the number of times the yarn is wound around it.

BOOKWORM BOOKMARK

Crochet hook   Any size
Yarn   About ⅓ oz, any kind

The bookworm in the picture was made with a size H crochet hook and 4-ply wool yarn.
Ch 15 inches.

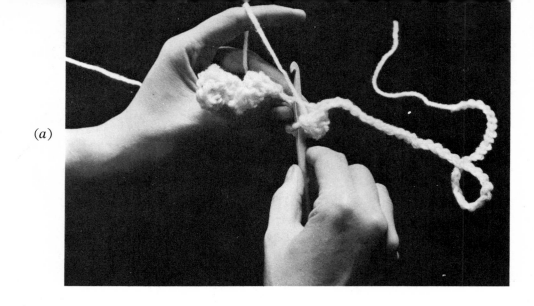

(a)

Do not chain 3 and do not skip a stitch. *2 dc in 1 ch st* 16 times. You have used 16 chain stitches and have made 32 dc. The remaining chain stitches are the bookworm's "tail."

Turn the piece so the chain edge is on top. Count back 3 chain stitches. Put crochet hook into this third chain stitch (a) and join with a slip stitch (p. 38), which will make a fold in the end of the "body." End off.

Make a pompon following directions on p. 52, using ½-inch cardboard and winding the yarn 40 times. Tie it to the end of the chain.

Make eyes of beads, buttons, sequins, or embroidery. Twist the bookworm until it curls.

This bookworm bookmark is easy to make. It takes only a small amount of any kind of yarn and makes a great gift. Try using 3 dc in each chain stitch to make a curlier bookworm, and try a tassel instead of the pompon. It can also be made from ½-inch strips of plastic; one bread wrapper will make two bookworms. Use a large bead or button at the end instead of a pompon.

GRANNY SQUARE

This looks hard to make but it is really easy. It is just a combination of some of the stitches that you learned in the sample.

The rows are worked around and around instead of back and forth and are called *rounds*. The same side should be facing you all the time. The first round is a small circle or ring of chain stitches. On the second round, instead of putting your crochet hook into a stitch, you will put the hook *into the ring.* When the directions say to make stitches "into ring" or "into space," you should put your crochet hook under the row of chain stitches, instead of into the stitches.

The directions will tell you when to add a new color of yarn. This will leave two short ends. If you hold these ends along the edge of the work, you can hide them by crocheting over them.

Practice with any size crochet hook and any kind of yarn. Do one step at a time and you find that you can do it easily.

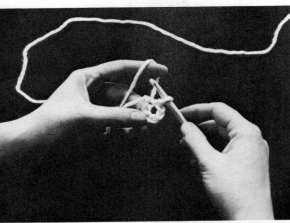

Round 1. Ch 6. Join to first chain stitch with slip stitch to form a ring.

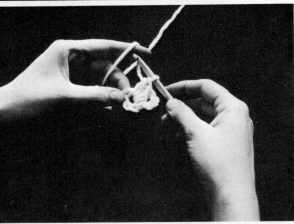

Round 2. Ch 3. (This counts as 1 dc). 2 dc into ring. (You now have 3 dc.)

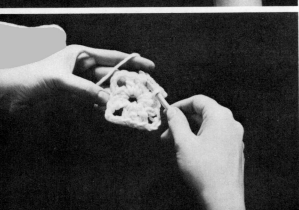

Ch 3, 3 dc into ring 3 times. Ch 3. Join to top of first ch 3 with a slip stitch. Cut yarn, leaving about 1 inch. End off.

Round 3. To add new color yarn, use crochet hook to pull a loop of new yarn through any corner space. Ch 1 using double yarn. Drop short end of yarn and ch 2, using only the new yarn. (This ch 3 counts as the first dc).

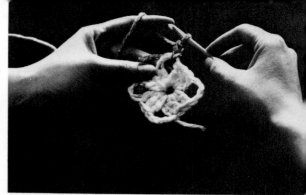

2 dc in same space. Ch 3, 3 dc in same space as the first 3 dc. (This is the first corner.)

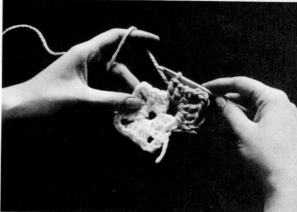

Ch 1, 3 dc in next space, ch 3, 3 dc in same space. (This is the second corner.) *Ch 1, 3 dc in next space, ch 3, 3 dc in same space* 2 times (to make third and fourth corners). Ch 1. Join to top of first ch 3 with slip stitch.

Round 4 and all other rounds. You can make granny squares with as many rounds as you like, changing colors whenever you begin a round. At corners, 3 dc, ch 3, 3 dc in same space. Along the sides, ch 1, 3 dc in each space, ch 1 before corner. On each new round, each side will have one more group of 3 dc.

Granny Square Hat

Crochet hook	Size H
Yarn	2 oz, 4-ply wool
Size	Fits most sizes

Make 5 granny squares, following directions on p. 56. If you use 4-ply wool yarn, 4 rounds will make a 4½ inch square. Crochet them together to make the hat, and work a border, following directions for hat on p. 48.

Granny Square Afghan

Crochet hook	size G
Yarn	22 oz, 3-ply wool
Size: each square	5 inches
completed	32 in x 62 in

Make 72 granny squares, following directions on p. 56. Sew or crochet them together following directions on p. 33 or 46. Finish edge with a few rows of sc, following directions on p. 42.

You can make the squares any size you like and use as many as you like to get the finished size you want.

Solid-color squares, single and double crochet, can also be used for afghans. Try mixing different kinds of squares that are the same size. This is a good way to use small amounts of yarn, but they should all be the same weight.

It is a good idea to use one solid color as a background. Navy blue was used in this afghan for the last round of every square and to join the squares together. It was also used for the border.

Granny Square Vest

Crochet hook	Size H
Yarn	5 oz, 4-ply wool
Size	12 inches square (fits most sizes)

Follow directions for granny square on p. 56. Work until squares measure 10 inches on each side. Make another square the same size.

Fasten yarn at any space and work 2 rounds of plain dc, making 5 stitches in each corner space to keep it flat. The vest in the picture has these last rows in different colors. End off.

For shoulder straps, with right side facing you, attach yarn (the color of the last round) to any corner of one square. Ch 3 (this is the first dc). Work 7 dc more. This will make 8 dc in the row. Work 8 rows of dc. End off, leaving enough yarn to sew shoulder seams together. Work another of these shoulder straps at the other end of the same side. Work 2 shoulder straps on the other square the same way.

Pin ends of shoulder straps together, making sure right sides are facing out. Sew shoulder seams, following directions on p. 33.

For ties, make a chain 40 inches long. Turn and work 1 row of sc. End off. Make another tie the same way. Use these to hold the sides together by pulling them through spaces as shown in the picture. Tie so vest will fit as loosely or tightly as you wish.

Care of Crocheted Articles

Crocheted articles made of wool yarn should be washed gently by hand in cold water and laid out flat on a bath towel to dry, away from heat and sunlight. Most synthetic yarns can be washed in a washing machine. See the yarn label for instructions.

When you have finished a crochet project, you may want to block it. You can also block pieces before sewing or crocheting them together. Blocking is shaping an article to the size that you want. It makes the work look flat and even. If you are going to wash the article, first measure the length and width and write the measurements down, or trace the outline on a piece of paper. While the article is wet, you can shape it to the measurements or to fit the tracing, or you can stretch it a bit wider or longer if you wish. Pat and smooth the crochet gently and allow it to dry.

Crochet can also be blocked by steaming. Pin the article to an ironing board with straight pins. Wet a cloth well, wring it out, and place it over the crochet. Then hold a *warm* iron (no hotter than the "wool" setting) close to the damp cloth, so the steam goes into the crochet. Take off the cloth and allow the article to dry before removing the pins.

WARNING: Be very careful when using an iron, as you can get burned by the iron or by the steam. *Never iron plastic.* You can block a plastic article by laying it flat and weighting it down for several hours with heavy objects like books.

Helpful Hints

A new piece of yarn can be added in two ways. You can tie a knot. A better way is to crochet it into a stitch. When you come almost to the end of the old yarn, cross it with the new yarn and crochet one stitch using both pieces. Then continue to work with the new yarn.

Hide ends of yarn by using the crochet hook to pull them through nearby stitches. If you use a smaller crochet hook than the one used on the work, this will be easier.

Measure crochet on a flat surface, like a table or the floor. Do not stretch it. Use a ruler, a yardstick, or a tape measure.

Fringe, pompons, and tassels are very much alike and are made very much the same way. If you need only a few lengths of yarn for fringe, it is easy to measure and cut them separately to the same length. If you need many pieces for a pompon, it is faster to measure the yarn by winding it around cardboard. Using two pieces of cardboard makes it easier to tie the yarn at the top and also to cut a straight line at the bottom.

Plan your work before you start. If you set aside enough yarn for your fringe, tassels, etc., you can use up the rest without worrying.

Keep your work loose, so that each stitch slides easily on the crochet hook. Be sure the thickest part of the hook goes through every stitch.

Keep your work and crochet materials in a bag. You may have a special bag for this, or you can use a shopping bag or heavy plastic bag.

If you do not have enough yarn of one color, use a combination. Stripes are attractive. Be sure to use the same weight yarn.

Never cut a crocheted article. It will unravel and come apart, because crochet is made of one long continuous thread.

If you buy your yarn in a knitting shop or a department store, they will give you free instructions.

You can find directions for other crocheted things in books and pamphlets in knitting shops, department stores, five-and-ten-cent stores, and libraries. Magazines have articles about crochet and have newer styles than books.

Glossary

Acrilan	a synthetic (man-made) fiber
blocking	shaping a crocheted article
cotton	a fiber made from the cotton plant, or thread or yarn made from this fiber
fiber	tiny fine thread twisted together (spun) with others to form thread or yarn. Fibers may be cotton, wool, or synthetic
nylon	a synthetic (man-made) fiber
Orlon	a synthetic (man-made) fiber
ply	a strand or thread that is twisted together (spun) with other threads to form yarn
rayon	a synthetic (man-made) fiber
rip	to pull apart crochet or knitting (unravel)
skein	a coil of yarn
spinning	twisting fibers together
stitch	in crochet, a loop of yarn
tapestry needle	large sewing needle with blunt end and large eye
thread	twisted fibers of any kind
unravel	to pull apart crochet or knitting (to rip)
wool	the fleece of sheep, or anything made from it
yarn	crochet material made by twisting threads together loosely